The poems in *The Willow Tree* by George Gott evoke the Tao Te Ching. They begin in simplicity and speak in the voice of a spiritual teacher. "Oh yes my eyes are open./Oh yes the dogwood./A thing of reality./The Lord is declaring/the blossom of peace." The lines have a spare beauty. Some of the poems' structures evoke rituals of benediction and praise and others contain questions we ask of life. The titles of the poems, numbered like chapter and verse, seem to be from an esoteric book of wisdom, perhaps a larger manuscript he still keeps. Gott speaks against war, violence and greed. Like ink drawings, the white space is as important as the clear and distilled images. Like a bell long after being struck, these poems ring.

—Sheila Packa, Poet Laureate of Duluth, 2010-2012
author of *Echo & Lightning* and *The Mother Tongue*

From Gott's invitation to the reader in his opening poem "Will you come with me/down one hill and up another one" to his assurance in the final piece that "All things will be revealed/in the blessings of joy" the poet leads us on a journey through shadow and through light, in language that is spare, precise and evocative. The poems in this collection are woven together with threads that challenge us, that call us to live our lives and create a world, not of greed and power, but of compassion and peace. "Why do they/scream at us?/The birds./The birds./They know/we will be making war/in the early spring."

These poems are woven together also with shimmering strands of hope. "Yet a fire within us/is speaking as if in a dream." I close this book, grateful to the poet for sharing the voice of the fire within.

—Deborah Gordon Cooper
Poet, *Under the Influence of Lilacs*

The poems of George Gott are as concise as Twitter postings but faithful to the traditions of Zen and imagist poetry. He gifts us with images that startle and excite while turning before our eyes the crystal of the world in the light of his vision. This is poetry of insights that cut below the surface of the contemporary human condition to connect us all with the possibility of compassion, and delivered in a precise tempo that has the effect of sculptured raindrops or the music of Debussey's Images.

—Dr. John Synott, Poetry Editor *Social Alternatives*
Queensland, Australia

I very much enjoy the poetry of George Gott. If one picture can be worth a thousand words, then the words of George Gott can be said to be worth thousands of images. His work is succinct and economical with an almost Zen-like quality. It can be accessible to all readers yet has a depth that satisfies and unveils to the reader the voice of a compassionate mind full of wisdom and knowledge using the poetic language of ordinary things and universal themes. His poems can be large and abstract as well as personal. "My father knew how to plough./One horse would do it/for a farm no bigger/than the boundaries of hope." I hope many readers receive the opportunity to appreciate the fine poems in his book *The Willow Tree and Other Inclinations*.

—Tony Fusco, editor of *Yale Medical Group's Caduceus*
and president of the *Connecticut Poetry Society*

The Willow Tree

and other inclinations

PRESS

A Superior Publishing Company

P.O. Box 115 • Superior, WI 54880
(715) 394-9513 • www.savpress.com

First Edition

Copyright 2011, George Gott

First Printing
15 14 13 12 11 1 2 3 4 5 6 7 8 9

Cover Art © 2011 Barbara Resheske

ISBN 13: 978-1-886028-93-7

Library of Congress Catalog Card Number: 2010943458

Published by:
Savage Press
P.O. Box 115
Superior, WI 54880
Phone: 715-394-9513
E-mail: mail@savpress.com
Web Site: www.savpress.com

Printed in the U.S.A.

The Willow Tree

and other inclinations

GEORGE GOTT

Dedicatio.

Dedicatio.

These are for Dorothy.

Always and always.

Some of these poems have been published in the following magazines:

Art Mag

Atlantic Pacific Press

Caduceus

A Conceit Magazine

Free Verse

The Laughing Dog

Old Red Kimono

Prairie Winds

Riversedge

Small Packages (Australia)

Turning Wheel

Social Alternatives (Australia)

Valley Micropress (New Zealand)

Woorilla (Australia)

The Worcester Review

Writer's Bloc

TABLE OF CONTENTS

ENERGEIA #013

Oh yes my eyes are open.

Oh yes the dogwood.

A thing of reality.

The Lord is declaring
the blossom of peace.

All things cohere.

All things lead
to the sunlight of happiness.

Will you come with me
down one hill and up another one?

This is my validity.

This is my virtue.

The voice
of the Lord.

The voice
of the Lord.

Let us celebrate
the luminous moments
of the vigorous earth
and the transcendent sky.

AQALANI* #0115

The pigweed is beginning
to bloom.

The pigweed has been
in the mouth
of the hog.

In the stomach
of the hog.

But that's historical.

The pigweed is beginning
to bloom
and all of the world
is celebrating
a harmony.

*Native American greeting

KYOKU #0595

Instantaneously
it happens.

A tick discovers
our body.

And the universe
asks us:
"Who are you?"

We live
in a world
of butterflies
and grasshoppers.

And ticks.

We do
as the stars
ask us to.

And we survive
in the constellation
of what we are.

ABZ #0386

Time does what we tell it to.

Yet a fire within us
is speaking as if in a dream.

We know what we know
when we know nothing.

And we know what we know
when we climb the sycamore tree.

We use each and every gift
as a subtle reminder
of earth and Pentecost.

The bread is the bread.

The wine is the wine.

And oh how we are satisfied.

As time listens to us
when the wind is deathly cold
and we beg for a day
in sunlight.

ABZ #0318

Fox grapes.

Fox grapes.

We were hungry
for fox grapes.

All winter long
and even in summer.

How we loved
to watch them grow.

And then there they were.

Marvelous.

And wonderful.

Tasting the heavenly
wishes.

Of the children
of paradise.

ENERGEIA #003

My father knew how to plough.

One horse would do it
for a farm no bigger
than the boundaries of hope.

One word was spoken between us.

And I planted the corn.

Is there something lacking today?

Are we afraid of the truth?

Are we afraid of the harmony within us?

My father would sing
on his way to the field.

My father would sing
on his return to his breakfast.

Is there something
we should be doing today?

You know it
my friend
as well as I do.

LES BEAUX ARTS #005

Let there be energy.

And let there be love
that has no ecstasy.

And no vice.

It is a formula
prophesied by Plato.

And confirmed
by Aristotle.

It is a poetry
that is pure science
and a pure exposition
of the soul.

It is Giambattista Vico.

We are with the mother
and the child.

There is no joy.

There is no sorrow.

There is only the faith
and the beatitude
beneath the cypress tree
that will be ours
when we desire it.

Source: Henry Moore, *Madonna and Child.*

ABBEXA #0171

This morning I met
two little rabbits
who didn't get out
of the grass.

My dog chewed them up
and left them decorating
my silent front porch.

Love oh love oh
careless love.

Are we like that too?

QUAESTRO #016

The river was here
believing in us.

The stars were here
believing in us.

We were as naked
as the searching mosquito.

Wicked.

And vulnerable.

We knew how to respect
the lies.

We knew how to tremble.

The river was here
believing in us.

The stars were here
believing in us.

And we thought
we could conquer
the world.

ABZ #0142

Why do they
scream at us?

The birds.

The birds.

They know
we will be making war
in the early spring.

When the columbine
whispers of sorrow.

When the clematis
trembles in fear.

Manitou.

Manitou.

Come down
from your mystery.

And prepare us
for living in peace.

ABBEXA #0145

That shadow.

That shadow.

It appears
in the sunlight.

Denying
the honeysuckle
and the dragonfly.

I reach out
to touch the vision
of my desire.

I am lost
in an ecstasy.

There is no honeysuckle
and there is no dragonfly.

There is only
my shadow.

ABZ #0288

Come with me
to Tamsworth.

The place of azaleas
and exultation.

Where once as children
we asked for forgiveness.

As if we had committed
all the sins of the world.

When the owls misled us.

And the hawks confused us.

Come with me
to Tamsworth.

And discover again
the place of exultation
and azaleas.

ASTROMA #0162

The stones
are the stones.

Giving us
recognition.

And sometimes
courage.

The foxgloves
may delight us.

Among the sunlight
and shadows.

The soul tastes
the manna.

And is forever
grateful.

And never lonely
again.

LES BEAUX ARTS #008

There is
whatever the eye can see
of unconscious affection.

There are no women.

There is an obvious arrangement
of two incoherent objects.

This is such
that it could never give us pleasure.

This is such
that it could never give us pain.

I am alone
with a thunder
that says nothing to me.

And I am alone
without a thunder
that would say nothing to me
as I walk away
with my loneliness
and an incomprehensible
anguish.

ASTROMA #0163

Ananda.

Ananda.

Do you not know
that we live
in abundance?

We taste
the holy bread
of salvation.

We drink
the pure water
of resolution.

Ananda.

Ananda.

Do you not know
that we live
in abundance?

ALLEGRA #001

She is with me now.

I speak of a dream
of loveliness.

The body.

The body.

I speak of the body.

The soul.

The soul.

I speak of the soul.

We have tasted
a breakfast of hope.

The Lord has provided
a feast
among the meadows
of our vast country.

Do you believe
what you see?

I see with my eyes
and I know that my eyes
are real.

I hear with my ears
and I know that my ears
are real.

Oh come our day
of Paradise.

May you be with us
forever.

LES BEAUX ARTS #003

She is alone.

A beautiful face.

A beautiful body.

And so lonely.

Did I tell you
she is naked?

Among the sorrowful columns.

In a city of magnificent
fantasies.

Ask yourself
my Friend
what have we done
to this woman?

Are we afraid
to embrace her?

Are we afraid
of a catastrophe?

Source: Paul Delvaux, *The Prisoner.*

ADOURA #001

We must choose
the one we love.

The perfect one.

The innocent one.

And adore her.

As the crocus
will assume
the beauty we share.

As the violet
will assume
the beauty
we share.

All human desires
would have perished
without her sense of courage.

All smiles would have disappeared
without her inspiration.

Let us go, Immortal Bride,
into the sunlight
that we discover together
with infinite concord
and harmony.

ABZ #0165

Emperor Bushido says:
"Let me show you the way.

"The way to heaven.

"And the way to hell.

"I hope you know
what I mean.

"There is summer
and there is winter.

"You can't quarrel
with a juneberry.

"You can't quarrel
with a snowflake.

"And you can't quarrel
with me."

We say:
"We know what you mean."

LES BEAUX ARTS #007

The beach
is not a beach.

It is the pursuit
of fantasy.

Sleeping bodies
disarranged
upon sleeping bodies.

I wish you
were here with me.

I wish you
were happy.

But I have
only
my imagination.

Sleeping bodies
disarranged
upon sleeping bodies.

Neither alive
nor dead.

ASTROMA #0215

In all things lovely
there is the beginning
of hope.

Whether I have had a dream
or not.

Whether I have had a vision
or not.

Whenever I have chosen
to climb the sycamore tree
and say to myself
I believe my eyes are seeing.

I believe my ears are hearing.

I believe my soul
is in touch
with the grain of corn
being nudged by the visible earth.

I believe you are here with me.

In the center of truth.

In the center of peace.

War has no ethos
to hold us together.

There is another Caesar
wearing a Cloak of Delusion
speaking an eloquent word
of corruption
giving us desperation and death.

Yet we know
what we have always known
as a child learns at home
there is the natural kindness
and the celestial benedictions.

ABZ #0311

Sooner or later
we realize.

A labyrinth
is a labyrinth.

As the American
duplicity
goes on and on.

Ignoring itself.

And strutting greatness
as if there is nothing else.

Except perhaps
economy.

We play with money
not knowing if it is
some kind of a relish
or a poison.

One must be so cruel
these days.

And to be so sure
that nobody notices.

As we create more enemies
and produce more weapons.

Yet we must remember
it is the gentle Buddha who says:
"Ye reap what ye sow."
"What ye sow."

"What ye sow."

So be it.

KYOKU #0324

The snake will survive.

Among the canna.

Among the bougainvillea.

The snake will stand up
and show us how to live
with that extraordinary courage
and the fear
of the Homo sapiens
and the bombs.

And we will dance.

In hope and in joy.

Among the canna.

Among the bougainvillea.

As love would have us do.

ABZ #0310

I learned to weed.

And I learned
to plow.

In the curricula
of the earth.

Then there was
a war.

And I learned
that death.

Is better
than life.

The flag.

The flag.

The flag.

And the beautiful
hysteria.

ABZ #0270

A thought is a thought
is a thought.

Leading to equity
or perversity.

It all starts
with a lily
or a rose.

What delights us
can control us
in the unshakable moments
of activity.

Be not deceived.

Even the process of joy
should be examined.

Joy without purity
walks to the slaughterhouse
expecting contentment.

A thought is a thought
is a thought
bringing about arrogance
or loving kindness.

ABZ #0306

Triumph is triumph:

It is the thing we do
upon a green of fancy
among the ghosts of Pentecost.

I was a hero once
for I had killed my enemy
but now I look him in the eye
and tell him it was love
that made me do it
in my lost sanity.

Triumph is triumph
as a bird is told
to never sing again.

And serpents awake
and greet the dawn
in pangs of victory.

ABZ #0266

Diophantus was enamored
with geometry.

But wanted no algebra.

And Diophantus was living
in the luxury of decadence.

It was a matter of politics
and religion.

See how we live today
seeking after ABC
and not XYZ.

As a matter of politics
and even religion.

Extremists have their day
among their theorems.

It is always the demonstrations
and never the results
that delight them.

They have created
the concept of an applause
that is completely certain
and absolutely unapproachable.

ABZ #0317

Queen Bess.

Queen Bess.

Was excited
by Ovid.

Believed perhaps
in prudence
and justice.

Some liked her.

Some didn't.

Lord Byron
was excited
by Ovid.

But that
was another matter.

Queen Bess
was dying
of politics.

America.

America
the beautiful.

We survive
in the lust
and psychosis.

ABZ #0283

Contradiction is always
a malignancy
in the visible world.

And the patriotic vision
is a cause and an effect
that is a matter of chance.

We kill and we kill.

We suffer and we desire
to promote it throughout the world.

For patriotism forgets two things:

First it forgets we are human.

Second it forgets that humans
have souls.

"La Verite c'est mon pays."*

Thus nothing matters
if we are exploiting
our heresy.

*Lamartine

There was once
the Pharisees.
And there was once
the Publicans.

As there was once
the Christ.

And now we exist
in a fantasy.

So be it.

For we have lied
to ourselves.

ABZ #0143

Someone must discover America.

Discover its dreams.

Discover its visions.

We are ready to move away
from the uproar of power.

We are ready to move away
from the affliction of the sword.

We must learn to see
with the spiritual eyes.

We must learn to hear
with the spiritual ears.

The Lord has demanded us
to join his handiworks.

The Lord has invited us
to choose the obedience
of the prophets.

America it is time
to take away the chains
from your people.

Allow us to live in peace
that is our gift
and our heritage.

ASTROMA #0164

The good tree.

The good tree.

And the apple grows
from the good tree.

Are we the tree
of hope?

Are we the tree
of faith?

We must become
the spiritual tree
that grows in the sunlight
in the world of eternal truth.

ABZ #0129

Yes
it is true.

And not true.

The snake glides
among the anxieties.

The anxieties of doubt
and the anxieties of faith.

The bird lives
without prophecies.

Singing nevertheless
in desire
and in harmony.

We look for a mountain
because we have been told
it is a place of ecstasy.

Or because we are told
we can live there forever.

Yet where is the mystery?

When the mystery is denied
the soul suffers the loss
and becomes afraid of the dawn.

ABZ #0395

Try meditation.

Try consolation.

Never attempt
violence.

Our rivers
are full of blood.

Our oceans
are full of blood.

The thorn trees
are weeping for us.

The green snakes
are weeping for us.

The past is not the present
but we cannot live today
in total mendacity.

The Buddha has said:
"Ye reap what ye sow."

And we are sowing the seeds
of vanity
and utter destruction.

ABZ #0390

Seventy-five years ago:

It was Franklin Roosevelt
speaking:

"I have an idea
I would like to share
with you.

"It is problem X.

"I hope you will agree
with me.

"And this is what I propose
to do about it.

"It is solution Y.

"I hope you will agree
with me."

And we were delighted
that someone saw a thing
very much the way we saw it.

Soon things slowly became better.

When the thoughts of the people
and the thoughts of the fellow in charge
were very much the same.

And that was democracy.

And it was taking away
our fears.

And it was giving us hope
and a dream of integrity.

ABZ #0254

What did Tiresias say
to Oedipus?

And was it something
Oedipus could have told himself
had he been able
to look into his soul?

I have said:

Soul.

I say:

What has happened
to our economy?

I say:

What has happened
to our politics?

What happened to us
when we became enchanted
with greed?

What happened to us
when we became possessed
with fear?

Isaiah suggested to Hezekiah
that he put his lands in order.

We must put our lands in order
for time is running out
and we must face
the singing winds
and we must face our destiny.

ABZ #0308

Infinity
promotes
infinity.

Seeking
the logic
of peace.

Never
the absurdity
of strife.

Kung knew good
from evil.

And all the great Emperors
of China
knew it too.

Knew how to avoid war.

Knew how to support beauty.

How to keep the people
tolerably happy.

Nothing in excess.

And all things supported
a liquidity.

Now what have we done
with sinceritas?

Now we no longer know
if we are alive or dead.

War is peace.

Peace is war.

And the Emperor of Dust
speaks in the accent
of weaponry.

ABZ #0293

Let us live
in the small mind
of the politician.

X = X.

Y = Y.

The earth
and the sky.

The clever ones
take our money
we made with our energy.

X = X.

Y = Y.

We live
and we die.

DEMOKRATIA

But let us ask:
Do our politicians know
what they are doing?

We have to awake
to the meaning of life.

The breath of the mountain air
will give us energy.

The taste of the spring water
will give us courage.

All things are becoming
a perseverance.

All things are believable
in the evolution
of a happiness.

ABZ #0399

The beauty of spirituality.

The beauty of science.

And there must be a unity
between them.

And we must remember
the flower does not ripen
suddenly.

It takes day after day
of sunshine.

As it takes the variation
of the falling rain.

And the unity becomes harmony.

And the unity becomes eternally real.

You and I awake
and we become aware
of the beautiful truth
that we discover together
in contemplation
and in the formula
that is the soul.

ABZ #0405

It isn't that we can't
do it.

It's simply that we refuse
to do it.

You can take a horse
to the water...

The rich are so rich
they live in a comedy.

The poor are so poor
they live without ignorance.

The politicians are so absurd
they live like Caligula.

His horse.

His horse.

And did he choose his horse
as his legal advisor?

It isn't that we can't
do it.

It's simply that we refuse
to do it.

ABZ #0403

The fulfillment.

The fulfillment.

Are we ready
for the fulfillment?

Where is the radiance
in the morning sunlight?

Where is the splendor
of summer in the garden?

I say to you little children:
Let us find the seed
of courage.

Let us find the seed
of harmony.

We sow and we reap.

Why should we live
in the past?

Why should we live
in the future?

Today is today.

It is the universe alive
and the actions we take.

We too are the earth
and the sky.

We too are the order
and the peace
and the convergence
forever.

ABBEXA #001

I said:
You know
who I am.

You said:
Yes.

I said:
You know
I am evil.

You said:
Yes.

As the earth
is the earth.

As the sky
is the sky.

I started
the ecstasy
of destroying you.

You said:
Yes.

ENERGEIA #004

If we seize power
we entertain the contradiction
of losing all power.

We are left in a desert
of cacti and affliction.

Jehova says:
"I am your god.

"Be not exposed
to the exotic winds
that will deny you
your heritage.

"There is the fire of love
and there is the fire of death.

"Know therefore
what I have planned for you.

"I am Jehova.

"And I am the word
of immortality."

AQUALANI #0150

We have faced the Tiger
of affliction.

One war
and then another war.

The False Emperor
smiles and smiles again.

He has brought about terror.

He has destroyed
the Hope of the Lamb.

Suwa. Segaltimaya.

Suwa. Segaltimaya.

We have made our great sacrifice.

What now is our heritage?

ENERGEIA #005

Shiloh.

Shiloh.

You were
my lover.

I was
your boy.

And I
was your man.

I functioned
in despair.

And I functioned
in defeat.

Shiloh.

Shiloh.

I was
your lover.

INVOCATIO #006

The world
you speak of
does not exist.

Does not exist.

This world
is one war
right after another war.

No time
for gentilesse.

No time
for grace.

We do
what we are told
to do.

We wake up
in savagery.

We fall asleep
in savagery.

ASTROMA #0181

Let us admit
we have entered
the world.

It is a world
that survives
in our prophecies.

Oh Lord of Truth
why do we quarrel
with our shadows?

Oh Lord of Passion
give us the knowledge
to love our neighbors
who live in the prisons
of our unrighteousness.

O Lord of Salvation
give us the power
to love our enemy
in the wars we have chosen
to celebrate our cruelty.

ABBEXA #0266

Yonder the bullet
is embraced
to settle our injuries.

Yonder and yonder
we know what we are doing
like the hawk
in the whirlwind.

INVOCATIO #001

How dreadful can it be?

I am told by twenty and twenty
there will be no money left
not even for the banks.

Not even for the government.

Bur surely someone will arrive
with the ordinary greed
and the extraordinary corruption
to feed the rest of us
with barley soup and sin.

Was there ever once
a depression?

We went to bed
a little hungry.

And we woke up
a little more hungry.

But with a thirst
even for hardship
that might come night or day
to keep the faith
in the invisible word
of honesty and truth.

ABZ #0307

We need a Secretary of Nature.

Soon I say soon.

So we can learn
how the grass will grow.

And we will teach
the children to sing.

Though we have lost
our innocence.

As we seek our fantasies.

We seek our visions
in our bank accounts.

And the seeds of madness
will not grow at all.

In America.

My America.

Until we water
our selected gardens
with our tears.

ABZ #0252

The Willow Tree.

The Willow Tree.

You are the image
that brings about a passion
as if the lute notes
were dancing with the wind.

I have known you
as I have known the flowers
of the meadows.

As I have encouraged
the seeds of joy
within my hands.

As I would invite them
to a new redemption
of the soul.

The Willow Tree.

The Willow Tree.

It is the vision
we have together.

And it is love.

It is the word of truth.

And it is the word
of harmony.

ASTROMA #0187

The Abundance.

The Abundance.

The fish
that is life.

The fish
that is truth.

The fish
that is love.

We must all
go fishing.

The Abundance.

The Abundance.

We inherit
the feast.

We inherit
the true identity.

And the glory
forever.

ASTROMA #0161

I am free.

I am free.

From the sin
that is death.

The Christ has made me
free.

I have tasted the sweet grapes
of salvation.

I am singing the glad song
of jubilation.

I am free.

I am free.

And I am living
in peace
and in harmony.

ASTROMA #0166

The manna
is here again.

Everywhere.

Why do we
deny it?

Why do we
indulge in barbeques?

The manna
is here again.

Among
the dying children.

Among
the living ghosts.

Everywhere.

And yet we see it
not.

ASTROMA #0141

Ananda.

Ananda.

There is no such thing
as a half truth.

A friend is a friend
is a friend.

Only in companionship
and loving kindness.

Ananda.

Ananda.

Either we are seeking
a life of purity
or we are seeking sorrow
and lamentation.

Ananda.

Ananda.

But you know this too.

ASTROMA #0142

If it must rain
let it rain.

If it must turn to snow
let it turn to snow.

The children will laugh
at the rain.

The children will laugh
at the snow.

Let us remember
we are the children
of the Heavenly Father.

If there is work to do
let us do it.

We will taste the bread
of gratification
and deliverance.

Oh Heavenly Father.

We will learn to obey you.

ASTROMA #0203

Annotations.

Annotations.

Have you taken the word
into your heart?

Have you thirsted
for the flowing waters?

Have you hungered
for the fallen manna?

The world offers us
various opportunities.

So much
that is dust.

So much
that is infamy.

I assume
my gentle reader
we know what we are doing.

We know when we are touching
the body of blessedness.

We know when we are saved.

ASTROMA #0164

The good tree.

The good tree.

And the apple grows
from the good tree.

And we are the tree
of hope.

And we are the tree
of faith.

We must become
the spiritual tree
that grows in the sunlight
in the world of eternal truth.

ASTROMA #0204

And the Lord says:
"Do no violence."

Let those who choose
to live in a wilderness
know they are committed
to belong in a wilderness.

So let us return
to the voice of the Lord.

So let us ask ourselves
if we have shed the blood
of the innocent.

The Lord has said:
There are good figs
and there are evil figs
and we must make a choice.

For the Lord has said:
Do no evil
for desolation shall follow.

Source: Jeremiah XXII, 21

ASTROMA #0173

Unity.

Unity.

It is at the center
of all things.

And the arrangement
of harmony.

Does the Emperor lie?

No one will ever know
unless we explore the truth.

The essence of doubt
is the beginning of understanding.

Ignorance is the hallmark
of order
and the beginning of clarity.

Does the Emperor tell the truth?

Does the Emperor indulge
In the Hieros Logos?

Some think so.

Some do not think so.

And who am I
to explain the difference?

ASTROMA #0231

The soul becomes active.

When there is a marriage
with the beautiful.

The beautiful is never
an abstraction.

And it is nothing else
but itself.

It has no subject
and no object.

As God the Father
is the creator of all things.

As God the Son
is the beauty incarnate.

As the Holy Ghost
is the obedient blossom
within us.

We rejoice
in the morning sunlight.

We tremble
in the falling rain.

We behold our reality
which is the truth
and the splendor
of the trinity.

ABBEXA #0165

It is so easy
to find fault
with the turkey vulture.

They are not beautiful
are they?

They are not polite
are they?

Would they stop to meditate
as they are pulling the meat
from the bone?

You have to admit
we do a much better job
of being politically correct.

We destroy our enemy
with grace and benevolence.

BENEDETTA #001

There are those which come:

To steal.

To kill.

And to destroy us.

Thus sayeth the Christ.

The sheep must be recognized
as the sheep.

The wolf must be recognized
as the wolf.

Here now.

As we rise up
and love our neighbor.

Each day.

As we rise up
and love our enemy.

As Jesus our Savior loves us.

Now and forever.

It is the truth of the ages.

And our gift of heavenly joy.

BENEDETTA #013

Let us remember
the Angel Gabriel
has said:

"All things are possible."

And we must live
in desire of holiness.

And in fear
of disobedience.

The trumpet
will sound
and our ears
will prepare
for the truth.

Our eyes will behold
the flowers of loveliness.

The asphodel.

The azalea.

All things will be revealed
in the blessings of joy.

For nothing is impossible
in the inclination
of the Lord.

GEORGE GOTT

Other Savage Press Books

OUTDOORS, SPORTS & RECREATION

Cool Fishing for Kids 8–85 by Frankie Paull and "Jackpine" Bob Cary
Curling Superiority! by John Gidley
Packers "verses" Vikings by Carl W. Nelson
The Duluth Tour Book by Jeff Cornelius
The Final Buzzer by Chris Russell

ESSAY

Awakening of the Heart by Jill Downs
Battlenotes: Music of the Vietnam War by Lee Andresen
Color on the Land by Irene I. Luethge
Following in the Footsteps of Ernest Hemingway by Jay Ford Thurston
Hint of Frost, Essays on the Earth by Rusty King
Hometown Wisconsin by Marshall J. Cook
Potpourri From Kettle Land by Irene I. Luethge

FICTION

Burn Baby Burn by Mike Savage
Charleston Red by Sarah Galchus
Enigmas by Fernando Arrojo-Ramo
Keeper of the Town by Don Cameron
Lake Effect by Mike Savage
Lord of the Rinks by Mike Savage
Northern Lights Magic by Lori J. Glad
Off Season by Marshall J. Cook
Sailing Home by Lori J. Glad
Something in the Water by Mike Savage
Spirit of the Shadows by Rebel Sinclair
Summer Storm by Lori J. Glad
The Devil of Charleston by Rebel Sinclair
The Year of the Buffalo by Marshall J. Cook
Under the Rainbow by Jay Ford Thurston
Voices From the North Edge by St. Croix Writers
Where Memories Dream by Steven Coz

CHILDREN'S BOOKS

Kat's Magic Bubble by Jeff Lower
Luella by Melinda Braun

REGIONAL HISTORY, MEMOIR

A Life in Two Worlds by Betty Powell Skoog with Justine Kerfoot
Beyond the Freeway by Peter J. Benzoni
Crocodile Tears and Lipstick Smears by Fran Gabino
DakotaLand by Howard Jones
Fair Game by Fran Gabino
Journey into Joy by Jill Downs
Memories of Iron River by Bev Thivierge
My Two Moms by Alice VanPuymbrouck
Stop in the Name of the Law by Alex O'Kash
Superior Catholics by Cheney and Meronek
Widow of the Waves by Bev Jamison

BUSINESS

Dare to Kiss the Frog by vanHauen, Kastberg & Soden
SoundBites, a Business Guide for Working With the Media by Kathy Kerchner

POETRY

A Woman for All Time by Evelyn Gathman Haines
Beacons of the Earth and Sky by Diana Randolph
Eraser's Edge by Phil Sneve
Gleanings from the Hillside by E.M. Johnson
In The Heart of the Forest by Diana Randolph
I Was Night by Bekah Bevins
Papa's Poems by Nick Glumac
Pathways by Mary B. Wadzinski
Philosophical Poems by E.M. Johnson
Poems of Faith and Inspiration by E.M. Johnson
Portrait of the Mississippi by Howard Jones
The Morning After the Night She Fell Into the Gorge by Heidi Howes
Thicker Than Water by Hazel Sangster
Treasures from the Beginning of the World by Jeff Lewis

HUMOR

Baloney on Wry by Frank Larson
Jackpine Savages by Frank Larson

OTHER BOOKS AVAILABLE FROM SP

Blueberry Summers by Lawrence Berube
Dakota Brave by Howard Jones
Spindrift Anthology by The Tarpon Springs Writers Group

To order additional copies of

Willow Tree

Call:

1-800-732-3867

or Email:

mail@savpress.com

You may purchase copies online at:

www.savpress.com

where

Visa/MC/Discover/American Express/Echeck

are accepted via PayPal